Play Ball!

by Larry Kelly

illustrated by Karen Brooks

Mike and Kevin like to build snow forts and throw snowballs. This helps them get set for summer. They like winter, but they think summer is the best season!

When the warm sunshine melts the snow, Mike and Kevin look for the baseball bags in the closet. "The mitts, bats, and cleats are still the right size," Dad says.

3

Mike and Kevin want to throw the ball around but not inside. Last season Mom's best lamp broke. Mom was not happy. After that, the rule was no balls in the house.

4

Mike and Kevin jump in the van.
They can't wait to get to the baseball
field. Coach Jim and players are
waiting for them.
Coach Jim yells, "Let's play ball!"

The day has arrived. It's game day!
The stands are filled with fans. The
team looks sharp in red shirts and hats.
The players and fans are excited.

It's the last inning. Mike swings at
the pitch and races to first base.
Now Kevin is up at bat. He hits the ball
and runs. "Go home," the fans yell.

Mike races to home plate. Can he get there first? "Safe," the umpire and fans scream! "This is going to be a great season," Mike and Kevin yell.